S0-BBZ-855

The Orphan Trains

by Alice K. Flanagan

Content Adviser: Becky Higgins, President,
Orphan Train Heritage Society of America,
Concordia, Kansas

Reading Adviser: Rosemary G. Palmer, Ph.D.,
Department of Literacy, College of Education
Boise State University

COMPASS POINT BOOKS
MINNEAPOLIS, MINNESOTA

Compass Point Books
3109 West 50th Street, #115
Minneapolis, MN 55410

Visit Compass Point Books on the Internet at *www.compasspointbooks.com*
or e-mail your request to *custserv@compasspointbooks.com*

On the cover: An orphan train on the Atchison, Topeka & Santa Fe railroad line arrives in Kansas in the early 20th century.

Photographs ©: Kansas State Historical Society, cover, 39; Prints Old and Rare, back cover (far left); Library of Congress, back cover, 13; The Children's Aid Society, 4, 17, 19, 23, 25, 27, 38; Jacob A. Riis/Getty Images, 5; Hulton Archive/Getty Images, 7; Jacob A. Riis/Museum of the City of New York/Getty Images, 8, 20; Lewis W. Hine/George Eastman House/Getty Images, 9; North Wind Picture Archives, 10, 16, 32; Bettmann/Corbis, 11, 21, 22, 33, 34; The Granger Collection, New York, 14, 18, 37; Courtesy of Kirk Pearce Collection, Lebanon, Mo., 26; Courtesy of KanColl and Connie DiPasquale, 28; Harold M. Lambert/Getty Images, 36; The Byron Collection, Museum of the City of New York, 40; Dan Herrick/Zuma/Corbis, 41.

Managing Editor: Catherine Neitge
Page Production: The Design Lab
Photo Researcher: Marcie C. Spence
Cartographer: XNR Productions, Inc.
Library Consultant: Kathleen Baxter

Creative Director: Keith Griffin
Editorial Director: Carol Jones

Library of Congress Cataloging-in-Publication Data
Flanagan, Alice K.
  The orphan trains / by Alice K. Flanagan.
     p. cm. — (We the people)
  Includes bibliographical references and index.
  ISBN 0-7565-1635-8 (hard cover)
  1. Orphan trains—Juvenile literature. 2. Orphans—New York (State)—New York—Juvenile literature.
  3. Adoptees—Juvenile literature. I. Title. II. We the people (Series) (Compass Point Books)
  HV875.F56 2006
  362.7'340973—dc22   2005025087

  ISBN 0-7565-1765-6 (paperback)

TABLE OF CONTENTS

AN ORPHAN'S STORY

On a sunny afternoon in 1930, 10-year-old Alice Bullis waited quietly for a train to pull into New York City's Grand Central Station. She was there with other homeless children. They were about to travel hundreds of miles away to start new lives with new families. As Alice climbed aboard the train, she felt "butterflies" in the pit of her

Boys head west on an orphan train in 1904.

stomach. She was excited but also afraid, thinking about what her new family would be like and if she would fit in. She wondered if she would ever see her real family again.

Three barefoot children huddle together for warmth in New York City in 1895.

The year before, Alice's mother had left her at a home for girls in New York City and had not come back. Alice was the oldest of five children, all of whom her mother had abandoned because she could not take care of them. At that time, Mrs. Bullis was a single parent without a job. She and her children were living in a tent in the forest. Alice remembered the days when all they had to eat were "wild berries and [muddy] water."

In the early 1900s, thousands of homeless children lived on the streets of large cities like New York, Boston,

5

and Chicago. Some of these children were orphans. They had no parents. Others had parents who could not take care of them. Between 1854 and 1930, more than 200,000 homeless children were taken to new homes in and around New York or to small towns in the West. The trains they rode to these new homes were later called orphan trains.

Alice Bullis rode one of the last orphan trains. Unfortunately, her ride to Kansas did not bring her to a happy home. Over a seven-year period, she stayed with three different families. She was ridiculed in one home and overworked in another. Yet Alice Bullis Ayler, who died at the age of 85 on June 2, 2005, was never bitter. She said, "Even though there were some bad times, it [the orphan train] probably saved my life."

POOR WORKING-CLASS FAMILIES

By 1930, the care of large numbers of homeless and orphaned children had been a problem in the United States for almost a century. It started in the early 1800s when people began leaving farms and moving to cities to work in factories. During that same time, more than 2 million people were arriving in the United States from other

Adults supervise young workers at a spinning factory in 1890.

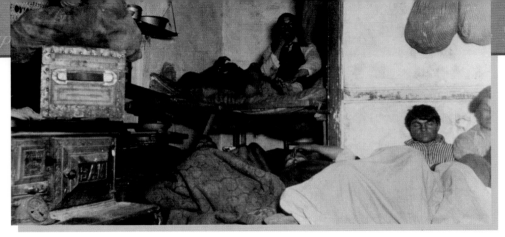

Lodgers crowded into a tenement room in New York City in 1890.

countries. The immigrants often settled in large cities and went to work in factories. Many of the former farmers and immigrants became the working poor.

Before long, neighborhoods became overcrowded. There was not enough housing for everyone, even in the large apartment buildings called tenements. The tenement owners charged high rents for small, dark rooms. To help pay the rent, two or three families sometimes shared the tiny apartments. The tenements—which were in dirty, unhealthy neighborhoods—were called slums.

People lucky enough to find jobs worked long hours under difficult conditions. Sometimes they worked 10 to 12 hours a day, six days a week. Often temperatures in the factory buildings were too hot or too cold. The jobs paid so little that workers could not afford to miss a single day, even when they were sick or hurt on the job. There were always other workers waiting to take their place.

Because there were more workers than jobs, wages were very low. Most working parents found it difficult to feed and clothe their families on the salaries they made. As a result, every member of the family had to help out. Some children worked long hours in factories alongside adults. Others earned a few pennies a day shining shoes or selling newspapers or matches. Younger children collected pieces of coal, scraps of wood, or old rags, which they sold or traded for food. In some families, older children were sent out or "turned loose" to live on their own. But even these children were expected to bring home money for their families.

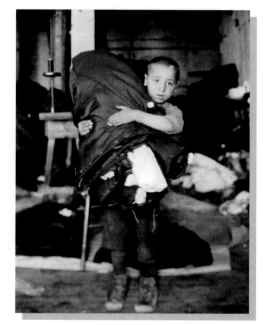

A young factory worker carries a heavy bundle of fabric in 1912.

9

NEW YORK'S HOMELESS CHILDREN

In New York City, where millions of immigrants entered the country, poor housing and difficult working conditions frequently caused illnesses and accidents that claimed the lives of one or both parents. If the children were not

Homeless boys sleep in an alley in New York City in 1890.

10

taken in by relatives, they were left on their own. In the mid-1800s, about 30,000 homeless children roamed the streets of New York by day. At night, they slept in doorways, under staircases, and in empty buildings.

John Brady

One of these orphans was 7-year-old John Brady, who later became governor of the territory of Alaska. Remembering those days, he said, "I would often pick up a meal at the markets or at the docks, where they were unloading fruit. At a later hour in the night I would find a resting-place in some box or hog shed, or in some dark hole under a staircase." During the day, John stole things and took them to a junk shop for money.

Although many street children, like John Brady, were true orphans, a large number of them actually had parents. Some of these children had run away from home because they were being mistreated. Others, like Alice Bullis, had parents who just couldn't or wouldn't take care of them.

To solve the problem of so many homeless children, charities began building orphanages to feed, clothe, and house them. By the 1850s, every large city had at least one orphanage. Unfortunately, most of them were large, crowded places in which children received no affection and very little education.

Not all the children who were taken off the street were placed in orphanages. Police often rounded up homeless children and put them in adult prisons and poorhouses. The law treated children age 7 and older as adults. If they were caught stealing, they could get the same punishment as adults.

In those days, children were treated like property. They had no rights. Without someone to speak up for them,

An orphanage in Charleston, South Carolina, was built in 1790 and housed more than 350 children during the Civil War.

they were often mistreated or forgotten. Still, many people were concerned about how children were being treated at that time. They said poorhouses and prisons were "the worst possible nurseries" for children. One of those concerned was Charles Loring Brace, a young minister.

HOW THE ORPHAN TRAINS BEGAN

The sight of so many homeless and neglected children in New York City upset Brace. So he and other reformers founded the Children's Aid Society (CAS) in 1853 to help the children.

At first, the CAS opened up shelters called lodging houses where children could eat and sleep. Each house provided clean beds, a dining hall, and a reading room filled with newspapers, books, and Bibles. Children were charged 6 cents for a bed and 4 cents for a meal. Six pennies also bought children a bath, a haircut, and new clothes. It allowed them

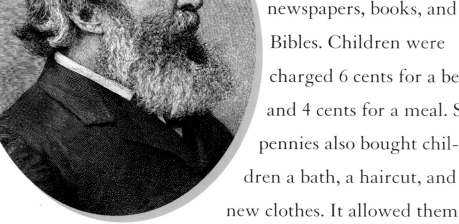

Charles Loring Brace

to use the reading room and attend evening classes, where they could learn reading, writing, and math. The children were charged these fees to help pay for the upkeep of the house and also to teach them the value of work. Schools were set up to teach such job skills as carpentry, wood-working, printing, dressmaking, laundry work, typewriting, crocheting, and knitting.

A year after the CAS began, Brace realized that children needed more than an education and a place to stay. They needed to grow up in a family. So he set up a program to get them out of their surroundings by sending them away to what he called "kind Christian homes in the country." Brace believed that the country was a safe, healthy place for children to live. He also believed that families who lived there would welcome children who could help with daily chores.

Brace's plan involved sending children to the country by train, because that was the cheapest and most reasonable way for them to travel. Several weeks before the trip, CAS

Nellie Brady, 7, was taken in by the Children's Aid Society in New York City.

After a day in the society's care, Nellie was cleaned up and wearing new clothes.

agents put up notices in towns along the railroad announc-
ing the time and date that a trainload of orphans would be
arriving. They also placed ads in newspapers describing the
program and asking people to contact them if they had a
job or home to offer a child. Then they sent small groups
of children to the towns, where people could choose the

16

child they wanted.

Before the train arrived in each town, a CAS agent selected a group of people to choose parents for the children. This group usually included a doctor, a teacher, a business owner, a minister, and a newspaper reporter.

The CAS wasn't the first organization to send children to homes in the country. This practice was done in England and France, as well as in the United States. As early as the 1700s, poor and abandoned children were

Homes Wanted
FOR CHILDREN.

A Company of Orphan Children of different ages will arrive at

Oakland, Iowa, Friday, Dec. 9, '04.

The Distribution will take place at the Opera House at 10:30 a.m. and 1:30 p.m.

The object of the coming of these children is to find homes in your midst, especially among farmers, where they may enjoy a happy and wholesome family life, where kind care, good example and moral training will fit them for a life of self-support and usefulness. They come under the auspices of the New York Children's Aid Society, by whom they have been tested and found to be well-meaning and willing boys and girls.

The conditions are that these children shall be properly clothed, treated as members of the family, given proper school advantages and remain in the family until they are eighteen years of age. At the expiration of the time specified it is hoped that arrangements can be made whereby they may be able to remain in the family indefinitely. The Society retains the right to remove a child at any time for just cause and agrees to remove any found unsatisfactory after being notified.

Applications may be made to any one of the following well known citizens, who have agreed to act as local committee to aid the agent in securing homes.

Committee: *S. S. Rust, E. M. Smart, A. C. Vieth, E. C. Read, W. B. Batler, Dr. R. G. Smith, N. W. Wentz.*

Remember the time and place. All are invited. Come out and hear the address.

Office: 105 East 22d St., New York City.

H. D. CLARK, Iowa Agent, Dodge Center, Minn.

Notices announced the arrival of the orphans.

Indentured servants assist a potter in colonial America.

being placed in homes to work as servants or apprentices. Sending children and adults to work for a period of time in return for food, clothing, shelter, and education was called the indenture system.

Although his idea of placing children in homes was similar to the indenture system, Brace's plan was different in one important way. Instead of treating these children as servants, Brace's "family plan" required parents to treat them as part of the family. In other words, parents were to give the young workers the same food, clothing, schooling, and religious training they would give to their own children.

The CAS called the program "home placement" and later "foster care." They called the parents "foster parents." Other organizations called their programs "family placement" and "out-placement." None of these organizations ever called them orphan trains. A reporter made that name popular long after these programs had ended.

A boy placed with a family in Texas rides his horse in 1903.

WHO RODE THE ORPHAN TRAINS?

The first orphan train arrived in Dowagiac, Michigan, in September 1854. It carried CAS agents and 46 boys and girls, ages 6 to 15. The children were successfully placed, and the orphan trains were off and running. They continued to operate for the next 75 years. From

Boys ready to travel west stand on the steps of the Children's Aid Society office in 1895.

Children clutch their dolls and bears as they prepare to leave an orphanage in 1918.

New York, some trains traveled west as far as California, stopping in towns along the way. Other trains went north as far as Canada and south as far as Florida.

CAS agents selected the children for each trip and got them ready. They made sure the children were bathed and given haircuts and two sets of new clothes. One set of clothes went into a small cardboard suitcase that each child carried. There wasn't much else to pack. The children were not allowed to keep anything that would remind them of their birth family, such as photos, jewelry, or letters.

21

Harper's New Monthly Magazine *praised the CAS project in 1873.*

22

Before boarding the train, the agents packed large boxes with sandwiches, fruit, and milk. They pinned a number to the children's clothing to help keep track of them during the trip. Clara Comstock, a very popular agent, made 74 trips on the orphan trains over a period of 17 years. She stayed in touch with many of the children she helped place. Years later, the son of one orphan said his father told him he sat on Comstock's lap "all the way to Kansas." He said the children also joked with her about her name, calling her Miss Cornstalk.

In the beginning, CAS filled the trains with children from its lodging houses and from the streets, prisons, and orphanages. That changed when letters started coming back from train riders describing the good life in the country. Then children began coming to the society by themselves and asking to go on the trains.

Boys like Marty Terrill, who was sent to Delphi, Indiana, in 1859, created interest in the program. He wrote about green fields, apple trees, and great swimming holes.

A group of boys on their way west in 1905

23

Some parents actually signed over their children to the society. They wanted them to have a better life than what they could provide. One father begged one of the CAS agents to take two of his three sons. He said, "I am sure, sir, if left in New York, they will come to the same bad end as their brother."

As a rule, more boys than girls rode the trains. Usually, the children traveled in groups of around 30. One time, however, a train bound for Pennsylvania carried 138 children. American-born children of immigrant parents made up the biggest single group of train riders, followed by immigrant children from Germany, Ireland, and Italy.

Although African-American orphans also needed homes, only a few of them ever rode the orphan trains. At that time, the majority of Midwest foster families were white and unwilling to take in African-American orphans. As a result, these children were left behind in poorhouses or orphanages for black children. Most Jewish children remained in orphanages in the cities, too, although there might have been more Jewish children on the trains than first believed. When they finally tracked down their birth certificates later in life, several orphans learned that their birth parents were Jewish.

A group of orphan boys posed for a photograph on their way to Missouri in 1908.

HOW ORPHANS FOUND HOMES

As soon as the orphan trains came to town, the children were taken to a hotel to eat, wash up, and put on clean clothes. Sometimes they even had time for a nap. Later, they were taken to a nearby church, courthouse, or hall where adults could select the children they wanted.

Orphans and CAS agents upon their arrival in Lebanon, Missouri, in 1909

A group of orphans was sent to Kansas in 1910.

Often, they were put on a stage so potential parents could get a better look. Children who were not chosen got back on the train and went on to the next town.

People had different ways of selecting children. Some looked for children with sweet faces. Others felt children's muscles and looked at their teeth. One woman chose a boy because his hair was combed and he didn't "appear half so rough as the rest." Usually, couples

A Children's Aid Society placement card

between the ages of 30 and 40 were the most interested in taking children home. However, single women and very old people took them, too.

Choosing a child to take home was exciting for foster parents, but it was frightening for the children. Being poked and questioned by so many strangers made most of the children angry and afraid. One orphan said, "I still remember what it felt like to stand there with everyone looking me over. It was awful. It must have been sort of like what slaves felt when they were [sold] off." Another orphan said it was like "picking out puppies at the dog pound."

For those children who rode the train with brothers and sisters, the experience was especially distressing. It was hard for them to say goodbye to one another. Most CAS agents tried to place brothers and sisters together. But because most foster parents only wanted one child, or could only afford one child, brothers and sisters were often separated and sent to different homes. That happened to Lee Nailling and his two younger brothers, Gerald and Leo, after their train brought them to Texas in 1926. They were chosen by three different families.

Some children who rode orphan trains, including Lee Nailling, were fortunate to become part of families who loved them. Their foster parents raised them as their own. Others were not so lucky. They went from home to home, without ever feeling they belonged.

When foster parents adopted a child, that child was

By 1910, the Children's Aid Society had sent children
throughout the United States and Canada.

given their last name. By making the child their own, they
became legally responsible for the care and well-being of
the child until he or she reached adulthood. When the parents died, the child was entitled to an equal share of the
parents' property.

Sometimes children were not happy in their new homes. Then the Children's Aid Society was supposed to find a new home or take the children back to New York City. Unfortunately, this usually did not happen. CAS agents tried to visit children at least every year to check on them. As the program grew bigger, however, that became difficult. As a result, CAS sometimes had no idea how the children were doing in their new homes. Most agents, however, kept detailed records of their placements.

During the early years of the program, CAS made it easy for adults to take children. Foster parents filled out a simple form, which asked them questions about themselves and their reasons for wanting a child. Then they signed a contract with the Children's Aid Society, promising to care for the child as a member of the family. Later, however, CAS required birth parents or the orphans themselves to sign a permission form before the society could place a child in a foster home.

THE BABY TRAINS

The success of Brace's orphan trains eventually encouraged other groups to start their own trains. In 1869, Sister Irene Fitzgibbon opened the New York Foundling Hospital. She was a member of the Roman Catholic Sisters of Charity of Saint Vincent de Paul and founded the home to care for

A New York City policeman in the 1890s holds an abandoned baby found in an alley.

abandoned babies. Often there were notes pinned to children who were abandoned. One note read, "God alone knows the bitter anguish [pain] of my heart in parting with this little dear. For God's sake remember the broken-hearted mother. Be good to my dear little Charley."

Nineteenth century hospitals and orphanages often had revolving doors where foundlings could be safely abandoned.

A few years after the foundling hospital opened, it began running its own "baby trains" to find homes for the growing number of children being left on its doorstep. Unlike CAS, the foundling hospital only placed children in Catholic families. And unlike CAS, it only placed children who were 6 years old or younger,

Sisters at the New York Foundling Hospital record the name of a new arrival.

and it found homes for them before they left New York. It also employed the indenture system.

The sisters asked Catholic priests in small towns to explain the program to their parishioners. Catholics who wanted a child filled out papers. They could even describe the kind of child they wanted. The sisters read each parent's request and then matched those parents with a child at the hospital. Then they sent a notice to the family telling them when and where the train carrying their child would arrive.

When the train arrived, the foster parents matched the number on their card with that on a card pinned to a child's clothing. After the match was made, the foster parents signed a receipt for the child and took him or her home. They were also given indenture papers, which had to be signed and mailed back to the hospital within a week. To make sure children were cared for properly, the sisters made foster parents agree they would treat the children as their own until they reached the legal age of 18.

THE END OF THE ORPHAN TRAINS

On May 31, 1929, the last CAS orphan train pulled into Sulphur Springs, Texas. A few homeless children, like Alice Bullis, still traveled on orphan trains after that date, but the agency-sponsored orphan trains had stopped running. There were several reasons for this. First, attitudes toward poor families and homeless children had changed by 1930. Instead of breaking up families and sending children away to strangers, organizations tried to keep families together. Laws were passed that prohibited taking children out of state for placement.

Poor children were more likely to remain with their parents by 1930.

The plight of the homeless had changed since a drawing of children warming themselves at a steam grate appeared in Harper's *in 1873.*

Also, new programs helped reduce the number of homeless and neglected children. Some of these programs helped mothers stay with their children. Others helped immigrants find jobs and housing so they would no longer have to abandon their children. As a result, large orphanages were no longer needed. Individual and small-group foster homes took their place.

Before long, the placement projects begun by Charles

Loring Brace and Sister Irene Fitzgibbon became a thing of the past. Because all of the train records were sealed, orphan riders found it almost impossible to learn who their birth parents were or where they came from. These family histories might have remained buried had it not been for the efforts of Mary Ellen Johnson of Springdale, Arkansas.

In 1986, while doing research for a book on the history of Washington County, Arkansas, Johnson read about an orphan train stopping in Springdale in 1912. She became very interested in the story and called Ethel Lambert

The remains of a Children's Aid Society poster

An early 20th century orphan train on the Atchison, Topeka & Santa Fe Railroad line.

for more information. At that time, Lambert was organiz-
ing the orphan train records and newspaper clippings that
had been stored in the basement of the old Children's Aid
Society building in New York City.

Johnson knew that the orphan train story needed to
be told. She began contacting orphans and recording their
stories. In December 1987, she and others founded the
Orphan Train Heritage Society of America to help orphan
train riders keep in touch with each other and locate their
birth families. The society preserves the stories of the orphan
train era so that the history, so long ignored, is not forgotten.

Now every year, train riders and their families—plus
historians, social workers, and genealogists—get together to

Although the orphans housed at the New York Foundling Hospital in 1900 are gone, their stories remain.

share their experiences and support one another. There are only a few known orphan train riders still alive. But their living relatives probably number in the millions. People can learn all about the train riders' experiences when they visit the Orphan Train Heritage Society of America Museum and Research Center in Concordia, Kansas.

For 75 years, the orphan train program was a solution to the problem of homeless children in the United States. It may not have been the best solution, but it kept thousands of children alive and gave most of them opportunities they might never have had. It also brought attention to the needs of children and encouraged governments to develop laws to help them.

Today, the Children's Aid Society and New York Foundling Hospital continue their efforts with New York City's children and families, working hard to improve their lives.

With the help of the Orphan Train Heritage Society and the stories of the orphans, foster care and adoption agencies will not repeat past mistakes. Their programs will help today's children understand, as many of the train riders did, that strangers can learn to love one another and families can form in many ways.

Senator Hillary Rodham Clinton (right) visited the Children's Aid Society, whose work continues today.

41

GLOSSARY

foster care—being a parent to someone who is not related by blood or adoption

foundling—an abandoned baby that has been found

indenture—a contract binding one person to work for another for a certain amount of time

orphanages—places that care for children whose parents are dead

slums—dirty, run-down housing in an overcrowded area of a city

DID YOU KNOW?

- Ethel Lambert found Charles Loring Brace's diaries behind old filing cabinets in a hidden closet in the basement of the Children's Aid Society building. She also found scrapbooks containing newspaper clippings and hundreds of letters from orphans who were placed with foster families.

- In 1874, during one three-month period, the New York City police reported that 90,000 homeless men, women, and children had slept in their stations.

- During the 1800s, most New York City tenements did not have indoor toilets or running water. Tenement dwellers used an outside toilet and hauled water from an outside pump to their apartments for drinking, bathing, and washing clothes.

- To help support the orphan train program, the railroads sometimes charged the Children's Aid Society cheaper fares. In addition, wealthy people sometimes paid for entire trainloads of children.

IMPORTANT DATES

Timeline

1853	Charles Loring Brace and others found the Children's Aid Society in New York to care for homeless and unwanted children.
1854	First orphan train pulls into Dowagiac, Michigan.
1869	Sister Irene Fitzgibbon, a member of the Sisters of Charity of Saint Vincent de Paul, opens the New York Foundling Hospital to care for abandoned babies.
1873	First baby train leaves from New York.
1929	Last official orphan train pulls into Sulphur Springs, Texas.
1987	Mary Ellen Johnson of Springdale, Arkansas, and others found the Orphan Train Heritage Society of America to help orphan train riders.
2005	Construction begins on the Orphan Train Heritage Society of America Museum and Research Center in Concordia, Kansas.

IMPORTANT PEOPLE

CHARLES LORING BRACE (1826–1890)
Minister and founder of the Children's Aid Society

CLARA COMSTOCK (1879–1963)
Teacher and popular CAS agent on the orphan trains

SISTER IRENE FITZGIBBON (1823–1896)
Roman Catholic nun and founder of the New York Foundling Hospital

MARY ELLEN JOHNSON (1939–)
Founder of the Orphan Train Heritage Society of America

WANT TO KNOW MORE?

At the Library

Cushman, Karen. *Rodzina*. New York: Clarion Books, 2003.

Goodman, Susan E. *Brave Kids: True Stories from America's Past*. New York: Aladdin Paperbacks, 2004.

Reef, Catherine. *Alone in the World: Orphans and Orphanages in America*. New York: Clarion Books, 2005.

Tamar, Erika. *The Midnight Train Home*. New York: Knopf, 2000.

Warren, Andrea. *Orphan Train Rider: One Boy's True Story*. Boston: Houghton Mifflin, 1996.

Warren, Andrea. *We Rode the Orphan Trains*. Boston: Houghton Mifflin, 2001.

On the Web

For more information on the *Orphan Trains*, use FactHound
to track down Web sites related to this book.

1. Go to *www.facthound.com*

2. Type in a search word related to this book
   or this book ID: 0756516358

3. Click on the *Fetch It* button.

Your trusty FactHound will fetch the best Web sites for you!

On the Road

**Orphan Train Heritage
Society of America Museum
and Research Center**
300 Washington St.
Concordia, KS 66901
785/243-2866
Exhibits of photos, clothing, and
other memorabilia from the orphan
train era

Museum of Transportation
3015 Barrett Station Road
St. Louis, MO 63122
314/965-7998
Large collection of vehicles,
including many train cars and
more than 70 locomotives

Look for more We the People books about this era:

Angel Island
ISBN 0-7565-1261-1

The Great Chicago Fire
ISBN 0-7565-1263-8

Great Women of the Suffrage Movement
ISBN 0-7565-1270-0

The Harlem Renaissance
ISBN 0-7565-1264-6

The Haymarket Square Tragedy
ISBN 0-7565-1265-4

The Hindenburg
ISBN 0-7565-1266-2

Industrial America
ISBN 0-7565-0840-1

The Johnstown Flood
ISBN 0-7565-1267-0

The Lowell Mill Girls
ISBN 0-7565-1262-X

Roosevelt's Rough Riders
ISBN 0-7565-1268-9

A complete list of We the People titles is available on our Web site:
www.compasspointbooks.com

INDEX

About the Author

Alice Flanagan has written more than 100 titles for children and teachers. Her books include holidays, phonics for beginning readers, career guidance, biographies of U.S. presidents and first ladies, and informational books about famous people and events in American history. Ms. Flanagan lives with her husband in Chicago, Illinois. As a writer/photographer team, they have published several books together. Their travels have taken them to many beautiful places and brought them many lifelong friends.